mind walking

Phoebe Caldwell

Beaten Track
www.beatentrackpublishing.com

Mind Walking

The poems below appeared previously in *Listening to the Landscape*, Fisherrow Press, 2021: Time Out of Sync; Rosa Canina (first verse); Teampull na Trahaid; Cairn Holy; Mute Swan.

Beaten Track Publishing,
Burscough, Lancashire.
www.beatentrackpublishing.com

Contents

mind walking

Absent Friend

Sometimes at night
before going to sleep
when I read poetry to myself
I want you beside me,
so I can say,
what about this one
and we can listen together –
and after the words have ended
we can go on
listening to the silence
that binds us.

Bull's Eye

She articulates each word with care,
follows its undeviating flight
arc through the air. The shaft
shivers as it strikes the target,
dead centre.

Her pen is a self-inflicted wound,
she had always been ruthless:
read my heart, read my heart,
draw out the meaning of astringency.

Arrow from the undermind,
now, to no future, is some trajectory,
retrospect and anticipation gone,
only in the act of dying.
is her quiver empty.

PHOEBE CALDWELL

Back Then in Innocence

Step back down the moving stair of time,

to the end of 'thirty-nine, before the Enigma code

was cracked, and wolfpacks roamed unchallenged,

sinking merchant ships at will.

Head on her bag, she sleeps on the warehouse floor,

embalmed in the smell of feet and fag ends.

Cigarette smoke drifts through collared light.

Hundreds of wounded soldiers wait to embark

on the Polish hospital ship, MS *Batory*. Aged seven,

she rolls the name round her tongue – even now,

'Gdynia line' – is a handrail from the past.

On board, she stands on deck beside her
    mum,

listens to the ship's captain speak to the
    troops.

'If you have to leap into the sea, tug at your

lifebelt, or your neck will break.'

She looks over the side, it seems a long way
    down

and wet –why anyone would want to
    jump?

Her mother nudges her. 'Are you listening?'

Must be important.

Day after day, the sea looks much the same,

restless shoulders of water climb and lurch,

climb and lurch, only deck-tilt alters shift.

Monotony detonates abruptly –

torn from nothingness to explosion,

standing start to the calico tearcrash

of sheering metal.

                                       PHOEBE CALDWELL

A sailor on torpedo watch
leans over the rail, looking for telltale
incoming trails, tells the child,
'No worries, we're catching fish to eat,
look overboard, you'll see.'

Stunned by blast, a pod of whales
floats belly up, uneven on the waves.
collateral damage to a submarine attack.

Two days on, disembarkation,
(mainline blocked, wartime priority),
the train trundles through worn-out forest,
saplings sag in pools of snowmelt:
journey's end with Dad in Washington.
Eight months later they are flying home
to an island under siege.

De-escalate to now:
the quick-witted sailor
who shielded the child from fear,
lives in present memory.

Museum Pieces

We have looted your sculptures,
put them on display in museums,
treated them with care, they are beautiful
– and we are amazed how primitive
peoples could have such refinement.

We have even exhumed the bones
of your ancestors: generations
of skeletons wait to be examined,
so we can write learned papers
about indigenous ways of life, as if
you are objects, not men and women.
What have we done?

PHOEBE CALDWELL

Hug

Dad is scything the field,

slow sweeps, parallel to the earth,

'Take care not to catch the tip,

buckle the blade,

you can cut your leg off with that.'

Even strokes – coumarin drifts

as stubble falls in rows.

When he stops to hone the chine,

I ask if I can try.

Not yet full-grown, the curving snaith

is awkward in my grasp:

my father gathers me from behind,

setting the tempo:

I feel the measure of his swing.

Snagging a tussock with the tip,

my cuts fall in awkward clumps,

testament to inexperience,
no good for harvesting.
'You'll need to grow a bit
to bear the weight.'

The field is sold,
Dad, long-since reaped:
his rhythm hugs me now.

PHOEBE CALDWELL

Birdsong

On the other side of the world,
you talk to me of birds,
the wild aviary in the tree out there
beyond the balcony.

The cockatoo is hungry,
squawks and lifts his lemon crest,
jabs the glass, letting you know
it's time for breakfast,
always with the or-else threat,
'I'll chew your window frames.'
The kookaburra laughs
as he stakes his territory,
chasing his rival off the branch,
jabbing him with his beak;
next minute he's making eyes at you
from the table. Hints of blue flash

from his brown wing feathers.

Do not be deceived,

he's also after seed.

All I can offer is a song-thrush

mimicking the ambulance in reverse,

Beep-Beep-Beep.

PHOEBE CALDWELL

Forecast

Weather on the edge of massive a storm,
not so much force ten gales but hosepipe
    drill,
deluge directed from directly overhead,
two months' worth in two days.

Wrap up tight, scarf, anorak,
waterproof trews, insulate
to the point I can scarcely move –
set off along the track.

Ground dry as a six-month bone,
no rings in puddles, not a drop,
cyclonic intention stalled, cardiac arrest
somewhere in Scandinavia.

Halfway round, a whisper of wind
twitches the poplar tree, brushes my cheek,
a raindrop writes its watery grieve
on tarmac under my feet.

'Question – shall I get wet? Hill rumbles –
auger of thunder or distant train?

'Actually, like the kiss of rain,
if it's not running down my neck.'

Moderation in all: no choice
but plenty of time, wet or dry,
turn back home: three hours later,
still no downpour from the clouds.

PHOEBE CALDWELL

There and Here

Sitting by the window
eating breakfast, watching
the news, I'm not afraid
when a helicopter
chunters past outside, it's not
shooting up pedestrians,
dropping bombs,
but on a rescue mission –
a climber in the hills is injured,
help is on its way.

How can I reconcile on-screen
visceral hatred, with the dale's
peace and quiet, the reality
of 'over there', with 'here tranquillity'?
Same lump of rock, orbiting
through different circumstance.

Then and Now

Triggered by today's events,
memories from an in-there hard drive
escort a postcard from the past.
'Then' melds with 'Present',
old data blown up by the add-ons
of never quite sure
when what occurred.

Experience of present embroiders
the definition of long time ago,
adds bricks to the Lego of child's play.
Flatland builds skyscrapers, falls into holes,
Elaboration pins spice to long ago,
makes it all less accurate,
more fun. Who cares?

After the Storm

Walls cling to slopes,

limestone hills slide into the dale.

Where I used to stand straight

and drink in the view,

now, bonsai to age, I'm bent

like a broken-back rocking horse –

examine the path in front of my nose:

where the scarlet drupes of rowan trees

and whirligig maple seeds

wilt on the ground.

How long before I lie down,

wither like them?

And will there be Presence or Sleep

in the landscape of death?

Watching Without Attenborough

No matter how defined the film,
it's different crawling hands and knees
in the afterburn of dusk,
trying not to crack twigs, hardly to breathe,
to crouch behind the bank and wait
until darkness settles.
There, can you see, there it is,
in the entrance to the sett?
A striped muzzle tests the air, hesitates –
and away. Its long coat bounces.
Pungency is absent online.

Pipistrelles nest in the flue of an old kiln,
a naked pup squirms over its mother's breast,
searching for a teat.
The camera will treat me to its quest,
but only in one sense; intimacy is missing.

PHOEBE CALDWELL

A raw banana draws the pine martin
to the sill, an unlikely preference
that lures it from the spinney.
A wild pony nuzzles my neck,
steals an apple from my pack,
an otter swims a mountain stream
on the diagonal, red squirrels leap
from tree to tree, kit tries to follow,
loses its footing, misses,
lands with a thump at my feet.

Sitting by a copse,
sunlight dapples faded grass:
the peace is broken by a horn,
hounds run down the far side of the dip,
fan over the field like spilt milk,
the hunt is up.
A huge dog fox breaks from the wood,
crosses the field. His coat gleams:
no panic in his stride,

it seems he knows he has already

lost his scent in the stream.

A confused pack,

snuffles in the undergrowth,

The huntsman calls them off,

todd continues over the crest.

Insects come in for a rough time.

Apart from ladybirds and butterflies,

the instinct is squash:

large as a flannel for a doll, no-one

could call an oak eggar decorative.

In temporary captivity,

she fires eggs hard as ball bearings

against the bell jar,

Ping, ping, on the glass. Her caterpillars

grow large enough to bump a bike wheel,

faded moths munch brambles.

PHOEBE CALDWELL

Now I am old, flash recalls

jostle the limbic system,

bang brainside: remember this?

And this? And this again?

Memories spill like a near-death cascade.

Such close encounters

reincarnate honed senses.

While entertained by TV hippo yawns,

wild elephants I'll never see,

raw meetings bond that then with now,

the natural world with who is me.

('Todd' is a dog fox.)

Teampull na Tranaid

Beathag, daughter of Somhairle
laid the first stone
In the name of God the Father,
Son and Holy Spirit.

There are no ghosts here,
only blind windows,
archways without doors, wind sough –
and for visitors, a metal plaque.

Perhaps the pilgrims
came from beyond the Isles,
not just to learn and pray,
but in this nettle-bed nave
to sit as I do, watching plovers
tumble blunt-winged from the sky,
interpreting their shrill cries
as silence.

PHOEBE CALDWELL

The Second Life of Shanidar Z

*(Shanidar Z is the name given to the remains
of a Neanderthal woman, who together with
members of her tribe was found in a cave in
the hills of Iraqi Kurdistan. Her skull has been
painstakingly reconstructed. The first verse
is largely taken from newspaper reports and
Netflix film on of the discoveries.)*

Skull crushed flat, fragments

separated from sediment,

bone – 'the consistency of dunked biscuit' –

flesh sculpted to her Neanderthal face,

standing brows and low forehead,

Shanidar Z gazes out with serenity.

Time lived apart,

but in the same world

her eyelids and mine have opened

to light and dark, sun rise and set,

moon peel, stars peppering the night,
comets streak, and drifting cloudbanks.
We have taken refuge from rain,
thunder and bolts of lightning.

She and her tribe have felt heat and cold,
warmed themselves with the pelts
of hunted animals, made tools,
cared for an injured child, carefully
aligned the dead in a burial site.
All this is known from her grave.
I cannot touch her,
but over the horizon of years,
her smile enfolds me. We are kin.

PHOEBE CALDWELL

Cairn Holy

The lane winds up through rhododendrons,
opens to a field enamelled with flowers.
Overlooking the sea, Sarsens needle the sky.

We are not alone, a couple with their dogs
have got here first. Out on parole, the Dead
    Man
has them pinned against the stones.

Unused to space, the spectre hovers,
flails his arms, lurches uncertainly
as he describes the claustrophobia,
running walls and cramped conditions
of his coffin. His hair
streams in the breeze,
shirt balloons, his restless bones
insist this audience understand
the significant alignment of his tomb.

Do you see precisely where shadow falls
in relation to the sun's orbit?
His words snag the solitude we sought.

He plays them on a leash, reins them in
when he sees them move towards the gate.
As they gather their hounds,
he glances sideways, sizing up
our potential. We turn away,
leave him all alone,
old man taking selfies of his history.

PHOEBE CALDWELL

Big Time Sort

End-of-life sortage, the urge to clean up

empties files overflowing with papers,

insurance premiums, house sales, enough-

to-choke-the-shredder confidential work
    reports.

While these are easy to dispose of,

it's making one's mind up on personal stuff,

which photos to bin and those

that have meaning for the next generation.

How about Great-uncle Bill and wife,

pith helmets askew, disembarking

from a boat crossing the Ganges,

and copies of Georgian portraits

from an unrecognised branch of the family?

Worst is to tear up old friends they never
    knew;

act of betrayal.

I envy my young, everything on line,
Easy-to-delete selfies, but they will still
have to make decisions.

Death of a Poet

Last day but one
she asked for pen and paper,
thought she might be able
to mine the darkness
one more time,
but thought stayed outside
the screen round her bed,
words had already slipped
into the void, page
remained empty,
nothing came.

For my friend, Enid.

Alert

Alarm pendant,
freedom on a leash,
no need to worry now,
or constant reminder
of frailty dangling
between my breasts?

Peace of mind
at the press of a button,
elderly release
by digital, or someone,
somewhere, has me
in their sights?

Forget fall, what I seek
is manumission
from antiquity,
the omnipresent nudge
that says, you are past
your sell-by date.

PHOEBE CALDWELL

Acer Pseudoplatanus

Leaves brush her cheek
as she walks under
an ornamental Maple.
She stops to look – the flowers
are almost invisible,
hidden in fists of foliage.

Never mind welcome shade,
the end point of this canopy
is to grab power from the sun,
synthesise sugars,
factory to build seed, wings
spinning like chopper blades
as they fly: prolongation
and distribution of species
is what trees are about –
as for all living things. For this
we bed and bear young.

Below Pultney Bridge

A swan stands on the shelf above the weir,
    squats,

countdown before launch, lowers her rump,

slithers forward on the river's slide.

She paddles to the side, clambers to a grassy
    ledge,

waggles her tail feathers, settles her wings,

walks sedately up the bank

and repeats her party trick over and over
    again.

Palladian windows yawn from Pultney
    Bridge,

they've seen this game before.

PHOEBE CALDWELL

Angus

Born a few weeks ago,
my new great-grandson
has the most delicious smile
I've ever seen.

It is difficult not to respond –
even to his online photo.
Hundreds of miles away
I sit here and grin.

Farvel, Copenhagen

Seeing she didn't have time to walk the
    streets,

she's little to declare, just a few vignettes

fished through the window of a twenty-
    kroner piece.

Cyclists sit bolt upright, pedestrians wait for
    green,

motorists drive through amber lights,

turn through traffic streams. A child

blows bubbles from a ring, watches canals

wobble in their sheen before they burst.

Church spires rise in tiers like wedding cakes,

a yellow spiral stair winding round and round

the finger pointing to heaven. Toy-town
    soldiers

square the circle on parade, the Baltic Bridge

springs to attention from the mid-sea,

    PHOEBE CALDWELL

upside coil of a serpent thrashing the waves,

the stuff of sagas leaping from the mist.

Far country.

Back home, she's on the other side of the
     coin.

Flint Beach

From sea to slip the creek wends through
    oyster beds,

flow fills to the brim, ebb empties to a trickle.

Black mud oozes through my toes like butter
    curls,

the smell of brine and iodine saturate the air.

A path along the bank winds between
    Tamarisks

(pink tresses brush my cheeks), past the seat

with its notice, 'Rest and be thankful

but do not throw stones from the beach.'

Adders warm by the stile.

Rails from the boatyard run down

to the head of the inlet; caught in sunbeams,

sawdust motes float inside the shed:

my eyes adjust to dim, to yachts

ramped up on props, while I listen

PHOEBE CALDWELL

to shipwrights at work, a symphony
of hammering, scraping, steam hiss.

Onshore, lightning has struck a flint,
a split eye gawks. Recognised
by metal buttons on his uniform,
flood washes out the body of an Excise man
buried in the dyke below the towpath.
'Do not stop at night to ask
the men you meet, why a light
is blinking out to sea.
They are about their business.'

Back to marshland, drifts of sea lavender
carpet the intertide, a lilac-on-blue mirage
merges with the sky.
Heaven should plant Limonium.

Grenfell Tower

'My heart goes out to you.'
That's what you always say.
Recently your heart must have been
clocking in and out like a cuckoo
as you see one horror
chasing another.

Does the River Thames hold sufficient water
to weep for my loved ones, my friends?

Charred icon, ill-clad
for a flamenco death-dance.
Finger in the air, monument
to good financial housekeeping,
cost-cutting interpretations, loopholes
and out-of-date building regulations,
casting a shadow over wealthier boroughs,
home to disposed families from all over.

PHOEBE CALDWELL

Now listen to what I have to say:

the stairwell was so packed with people,

it took twenty minutes for me and my little
    girl

to grope our way through the smoke

from my flat to the floor immediately below.

Two flights, one storey, I tried to hold on,

lost her, went back, she was gone.

So tell me, River, is it raining upstream,

is there enough water for our tears?

Firefighters sift through melted plastic,

dismembered kitchens, fused possessions.

Sniffer dogs search for remains.

Order now, order, use my shrivelled heart

as gavel to set straight the fretwork of
    despair.

Turn back the tide,

search hindsight for a clean slate.

Ernst Haeckel

Never heard of him.

Architectural drawings
of spiked jelly blobs,
unicells in full dress,
armoured in ornamental
helmet and cuirass,
trailing filaments, waiting
to entangle debris.

Test bed:
was this particular ridge
on the brassard meant
or accidental? And how many
designs came to dead ends,
evolutionary failures?

PHOEBE CALDWELL

No matter – exquisite depictions:
bring back my microscope,
see it aux naturel again.

*(Ernst Haeckel. Biologist and Artist.
Contemporary of Darwin.)*

Lift-off

St John's Halifax: land and sea
knit by rain, a Sunderland waits
in the harbour, dinghy
takes us to board.

Doors close, engines rev,
propellers turn,
she faces to the wind,
edges forward, slowly at first,
picks up speed, floats splay
translucent fans of seawater
as they slice the waves
on the way to lift-off.

A twelve-hour flight:
who can say these days,
they have crossed the Atlantic
in a flying boat?

PHOEBE CALDWELL

Eighty years on,
the child still remembers
those opalescent curtains,
waving goodbye.

Holding Silence

Half five, go for a walk

through sleeping cottages uptown,

no cars, no jostle as I pad

through silent lanes in the cool

before sunshine burns the dale.

Coming downhill, the air

is heavy with the smell

of lilac and honeysuckle.

I pause to sniff a deluge of wisteria

draped across the shoulders of a shed.

The first vendors are arriving

in the square, bagging pitches,

setting out their stalls,

pausing to drink cups of tea

before the market opens,

shoppers arrive trailing wheelie bags.

PHOEBE CALDWELL

Give me a cloister for my ears:
wrap my head in silence,
hoping to reach home before
the unfiltered Muzak of daytime
takes possession of space.

Growing Old Creaky

What happens when joints
lose their padding?

We are all beginners
when it comes to arthritis,
can only observe and surmise,
watch horizons foreshorten
as cartilage crumbles and spine
bellyflops into its pelvic cradle,
eclipse of relative positions,
point of view shifted, floor
closer, ceiling further up there.

Not only leaning, the tower of Pisa
crumbles as its mortar, subsides
floor by floor – nearly vertical
to a pile of rubble, while you're still
worried about that first wrinkle:
a time bomb lurks round the corner.

PHOEBE CALDWELL

Keeper of the Tide

She has a harvest of stones by the bathroom
    wall

gleaned from the rocky beaches of her
    wanderings.

Ground to pebbles by the endless shift and
    kiss

of sea waves, her shoreline is dry and dull

until each morning when she takes
    a shower:

the tide returns and laps their parched
    faces.

Moon on the wane, she waters granite
    cheeks,

washes crystals of alum renewing their shine.

In gravity she polishes her cobbles,
    lamplighter

to crushed garnet and serpentine

but for all her orbiting she cannot claw back
her own worn flesh at the turn of a tap.

*(Stones collected before they became an illegal
harvest.)*

PHOEBE CALDWELL

Ivana Gavric Dress Rehearsal

Ivana Gavric,

part music, partly mind,

the keyboard her battleground,

a pride of sprung steel fingers

flicker over the keys,

animals celebrating

and making love to their prey.

The notes twist and turn,

a murmuration of sound lifts,

hovers on the edge of the dive,

the auditorium holds its breath.

Wrapped in her art

we follow her over the cliff.

Foxup

A humpback bridge crosses the beck,
I slide myself down feet first,
grip the waterworn stones,
follow upstream to the source.

The clough bends, crosses a narrow pool,
I scramble up a cascade on the far side,
surprise a heron fishing in the bog.
He spreads his wings, leans forward, takes off
slowly, jumbo jet – will he clear the swamp?

The door bangs in a derelict barn, come-in
invitation to explore. Shaped like a crucifix
a window looks down the dale.
Had it been an isolated monastery?

The farmer, laughs, 'It's pretty new –
some years back, squatters got religion,'
he shrugs. But God or not,
the view from up there is paradise.

PHOEBE CALDWELL

Pipping Geese

Emdens are heavy, careless with eggs,
can't count, roll them out of the nest,
forget, so we bring them inside to hatch
on the stove, hear them talk in their shells
and they answer our calls, squeak
before pip, before the shell splits.

The crack widens, knob on the nose
eases a couple of flakes. Unsteady
on their shanks, a gosling clambers out,
takes time to fluff.

An animated pussy willow
starts to peck anything looks like
a blade of grass, even the tassels
on a dressing gown – once outside
it will be a vital wire
hanging down under the car.

Adult geese will care for their young,
take them up on the hill, stand guard
while they eat. I've even seen
the flock encircle a terrified fox
trying to break out –
and chase a delivery man
armoured with helmet and cosh.

Turn round, lower your head,
flap your arms and hiss,
you are a bigger goose than they are,
they'll run.

If the gate is left open,
they return to the kitchen. This
is where they were born, their place.

We hear their feet slap on the flags:
part of the family, inquisitive heads
pop up by our plates, look
what's for dinner. A visitor said,
'Don't you ever feel under siege?'

PHOEBE CALDWELL

I loved my geese, all seventy-six,
had to sell when my husband died:
grief climbed in the van with them –
I turned away and wept.

('Pipping' is the word for hatching poultry.)

Mourners

Mostly they come in twos and threes,
friends and family wanting to say goodbye,
strangers needing to be part of the departed,
clutching flower and soft toys,
adding plastic wrapped roses, mixed bunches
and balloons to the pile against the wall:
the weird take selfies at the scene.

What with terror and catastrophe
custom has blossomed for the florists:
stand back and consider your offerings
and the meaning of life lived,
now teddy bears are symbols of life lost.

Origin Story

Written by men, the book of Genesis
sets up schoolboy misogyny,
from patronage to sexism by right:
Eve comes out second class.

Searching for fig leaves, Adam
breaks down under cross-examination,
shifts the blame,
'She did it, it was all her fault.'

Discord sown, the serpent
twines round his branch,
laughs until he nearly falls off.

All in all, a good day's work,
embedding dissent in union
should bring on heartbreak:
male point of view condones
the marginalisation of woman.

Calligrapher

My sister teaches me how to write,
loop the loop between tracks;
my nib splutters.

The teacher at school
throws out my cursive script,
Times Roman now; bold and upright.

My sister shows me how to ride a bike,
one shove off; fall in the nettles,
no sympathy, get up, try again.

Introduces my fingers to QWERTY, gives me
my first cigarette. 'Draw the smoke in,'
laughs when I choke.

Now dead, she leans over my shoulder,
chooses words – not this one, that –
thesaurus and friend.

PHOEBE CALDWELL

Amazon

Night after night they come,
streams of emails
based on my browsing history
'Are you looking for...'
'You might like to know...'

You bind me in the silken threads
of your pitch; just because
I ordered once, shall I continue
in desire, need, possibility;
a non-emergent imago
trapped inside your algorithm.

I wriggle inside my cocoon.
If you continue long enough
you never know, I might,
just might give in.

Candidate

The candidate is robed in scarlet gown,
    practised hands

twitch the hood, and a hat with golden lure.

She is paraded to the Hall like a bride:

escorted, she is alone.

Carrying a rod of ebony, the Bedel pauses,

turns, sees she is ready and with measured
    stride

moves up the aisle. She walks behind, head
    bowed,

mesmerised in a ceremonial bubble, only
    partially aware

of the ripple of eyes breaking over their
    procession.

Seated by herself in front, she fills the row of
    empty chairs

with the people who have brought her here.

Day after day, Pete draws cats with staring
   eyes,

cries out, 'You don't know what it's like,

You don't know what it's like.' Bill eats the
   tulips

from the coffin of his friend. Mike shouts,

'We used to have walls in here.'

Uprooted from the nurses' garden,

Raymond offers me a rosebush in full
   bloom:

blood and soil trickle down his arm.

She watches the graduation: hatchlings to
   imagines

fluttering across the stage, the quick hand
   embrace,

words of congratulation from the chancellor,

launching each graduate with care into an
   uncertain world.

It is done. After party time, what will become
   of them?

The Bedel summons her. Mounting the stair,

she sits and listens to the Orator

running a highlighter through days that
 seemed

ordinary at the time, expediency

playing catch-up with the odd, one lifetime

squeezed into a ten-minute slot. Stories

drift across the stage, the speaker turns,
 smiles

and doffs her hat; the candidate rises,

holds out her hands for enfolding.

Honour is conferred by power invested in
 a gown

crusted with gold and worn with grace.

She signs the book, hugs the Orator.

Sweetness and poignancy. The scroll she has
 eaten

will take time to be part of her.

PHOEBE CALDWELL

Two Men Called Dad

There are two men called Dad, Home Dad,
   my father,

and Hero Dad, away in chest-medals
   uniform:

the latter mostly known from photographs,

standing beside an aeroplane, ranging

from Tornado to early bits of wood and
   string.

An unlikely warrior, joined up in the First
   World War,

from art college, served in the trenches,

sitting in mud, sheltered behind mounds of
   dead

mended a broken gun, placing the screws in
   his upturned cap

to keep them clean. Wounded, afraid of being
   overrun

and bayoneted, he crouched in a crater.

Rescued and sent home:

I've seen entry and exit bullet scars in his
    thigh, missed the bone.

Artist manque, the sky was his medium,

he enlisted in the fledgling RFC,

almost by accident became chief test pilot,

worked on how to bottom out of spins,

deliberately flew his plane into balloon cables

to see if modified wings would wrench away.

In the days when navigation followed railway
    lines,

(turn left by the Goring Gap), his fellow
    pilots crashed.

My mother, Helen, stood by, watched from
    the airfield,

could not bear to wait at home.

And so on, up the ranks. Another war,

Hitler's secret weapons, V1 Buzzbombs

slow descent: without consent, my dad

removed the guns from London to the coast,
saved its streets.

When he could no longer fly, he left the Air Force,
bought a boat, learned to sail
round Chichester harbour: became
Home Dad, standing on the backdoor step,
taught me to watch the sky, forecast rain
avoid flying into thunderclouds.

He divided the attic table with a rule,
that side his, this mine, showed me
how to draw proportions, Leonardo's
silhouette stretched his limbs in the round.

And he laid out lines to bring depth
through perspective to drawings.

Before I slept, he taught me poetry,
on the one hand Shakespeare's call to arms
at Agincourt, on the other, Robert Bridges',

'Testament of Beauty' –

> *we sail a changeful sea of halcyon days and storm*
> *and when the ship laboureth, our steadfast purpose*
> *wavereth, like to a compass in a binnacle –*

Much like his life, good days and bad.

Courage and culture, two dads in one,

I am grateful to be their-his child.

PHOEBE CALDWELL

True or False

Time warps the brain,
what happened, if it did, and when;
incidents with images hold fast.

While the child sits at her desk,
King Knut waits by the sea,
watching the tide creep in
to lap his feet, ripple by ripple,
kiss by kiss, turn back
at his command, irrespective
proof of his majesty, not.

Attention drifts, Alfred
burns the cakes, in her class,
she sniffs the blackening crusts.
And Robert the Bruce in his cave
heeds the persistent spider
spinning silk to mend her web,
over and over again.

Sadly, Nero never played

his violin while Rome burned;

stringed instruments were not around.

True or false, her brain

hangs on to facts with pictures,

clothes-hooked into time.

Blended Learning

My tutor's office smells of fusty books,
half-drunk cups of tea and speculation,
associations peeling off the wall.
'Look at this…' Have you thought…?'
and 'What about…?' mutual exploration,
pass me that journal, put the kettle on,
professorial interrogation, his delight
in a mind coming live,
mine at star-burst perspectives.

Cerebral crossroads: where should I find
such inspiration in the bland face
of asynchronous learning?
In a diet stripped of provocation,
adjusted to remove offence
tell-me-what-I-need-to-read articles
providing safe space, assurance.

A gag on interpretation,

tames the wild river of words:

no spillage, no chance to wake to ideas

gathered like birds layering their feathers,

preening in gilded spray before they fly.

Contingency denied,

the runaway fuse of presence is unfired.

Spillage

Midnight, need a drink,

trip on the way back to bed,

spill it over a pile of Christmas cards

waiting to be answered.

Wet greetings soaked in camomile

stick together, curious adhesions,

a woman with a flute plays

to a horned beast rising from the mire.

The emblems have shifted

from stable scenes to icy landscapes,

dogs with lolling tongues,

birds – particularly puffins –

and a personalised (my name, all mine),

Christmas pudding decked with holly.

One Father Xmas, rescued from the sea –

four soaking reindeer sitting in their sleigh,

bounce behind the lifeboat.

His clothes are drying on the radio mast.

Three Magi on the way, few Nativities,

although one cannot better,

'Adoration' by Filippo Lippi.

Prised apart, the images are spoiled,

but came with love – still need a reply.

Eruption

Tectonic shift, ground quakes,

pots clatter from shelves,

cracks zigzag the roads,

fingers spread labial fissures,

tongues of molten rock

explode from earthcore,

fire streams engulf the land:

Iceland reminds us of instability,

that terra firma can be moved.

Flight Path

A flock of starlings rain from the sky,
corpses litter the lane like fallen leaves.

So why did you not pull out of the dive,
continue to plunge headlong to earth?

No more wingtip wheel in ecstasy
of murmuration, shadow shift

across evening: the pendulum stops
under the shadow of the hawk.

Life Span

From birth to death,
infant to nursery,
child looking ahead,
uniform, schoolgirl, college,
work, falling in love,
marriage, and children,
grandkids, even great.

Bell curve, up the hill
and down, take a good look
at the view from the top,
doesn't come twice.

Signed-in to stretched-out span,
life seemed cosmic when it began,
but it's just a short slot
on temporary sub,
planet orbiting the sun
long after you've gone.

Railway

You can see where the ice cap passed,

sharp claws dragging rocks in its flow.

Engineers stub the map:

from here to here, we'll take the line

from Settle to Carlisle.

Workers live onsite. On Sundays

gather to hear itinerant preachers

spread the Word, weekdays,

lay track over fallen navvies,

bury them in the mire.

The woman is here before the viaduct,

stands under the ice wall,

burns her face on its frozen embrace.

Melt water flows from her body heat,

stream source still stumbling

PHOEBE CALDWELL

over jagged stones. With her hands
she moulds moraines in place,
quilts mud and rubble into mounds.
Drumlins roll below Ribblehead.

(From a watercolour by Philippa Troutman.)

M5

Message on the phone: urgent appeal
to excavate the burial site
before diggers arrive and tear it apart.

Scraping through sediment,
there she lies, abraded bones,
no necklace or beads, not even
a pot for use in the afterlife,
anonymous skeleton,
A. Woman,
curled at the bottom of the pit.

Reburied in a nearby church,
her torn-out shade spelt 'anonymous'
hovers above the carriageway.
Catalogued in the curator's list,
as in life, invisible in death:
no northbound driver knows she lived here,
this was once her place.

PHOEBE CALDWELL

Proving a Point

'Jump,' they say,
'if you want to learn to kayak,'
so she leapt overboard,
into the slate-green deep,
knowing she could not swim,
and sank, down, down. Her legs
bicycle, fingers claw the water
as she watches flattened bubbles
wobble to the surface.

Next she knows, she's retching onshore.
When she can speak, she says,
'Told you so, you didn't believe me, did you?'

Stupid really, sometimes she walks
thoughtlessly into the known unknown,
anything to prove a point.

Second Best

Wisteria smothers
the south-facing wall,
lavender muffler –
an effervescence of flowers
drowns the pebbledash.

A stranger knocks, blurts,
'Yours is the second-best
vine in the parish.
Mine is bigger.'
Mission accomplished,
she turns and leaves
without another word.

Put in my place,
I close the door,
ponder an inferior status.
Hope she feels good.

PHOEBE CALDWELL

The Link

Three years old, the child in me
sits by a bagatelle board, turns and laughs
out of the photograph, her seamless flesh
unsullied by the exigencies of years.

Over the hump, I answer her gaze –
bent like a hoop, triangulated on a stick,
my face graved deep, raised relief map
    gouged
with the ups and downs of circumstance.

From here I ask, 'Can I, the self
I feel myself to be, really have been, be you,
you me?' Then to now: what happened
to the me-we-are in between?

Password

Such a simple thing,
forgotten my password
can't get online –
my unblinking screen
stares back.

And I can't recall
my card number,
have to unpack
at the till. A restless queue
shuffles behind me.

Worse still, at the Pearly
Gates, I've no idea
of the code: dead
to the world down there
and up here
in a limbo of eternity.

PHOEBE CALDWELL

Second Hand

Description: euphemistic.

Paperback,
condition good to fair.
For real: creased covers,
page corners bent
to tell you where you were.
Sticky in places,
dabs of marmalade
wiped off page fifty-nine,
toast crumbs in gutter:
breakfast spilled
in the denouement.

Good story, not surprised
you couldn't put it down.

Mute Swan

The pen waterproofs her plumage with care, sorting

splayed feathers, setting each in order, zipping up strays.

She preens with diligence, pauses only to twist

her long neck back and scoop oil from her purse.

Her toilet ended; she stretches, shakes out pinions like spinnakers,

captures the breeze, surfs downwind: there is nothing more serene.

Give me wings, not just to fly but fill my sails

and glide to leeward on a silent sea.

PHOEBE CALDWELL

Freedom

If I should die, no,
when I am released,
all that I know
decanted into earth,
(arm withdrawn,
sleeve emptied),
is there afterwards –
and if so,
does this stretch
into eternity
or is it forever now:
present imperative?

Halt!

De-escalation,
Slow Down,
Unwind,

Full   .

PHOEBE CALDWELL

Moon Time

First the excitement, getting up
in darkness, opening the back door
slipping out without waking the family,
taking a footpath to the creek;
every blade of grass
defined by moonlight.

Stand on the bank – look at the contrast,
passive shine from mudbanks,
wound through by ripples of incoming tide.

Look at myself: arm glazed argent,
stilled by her purity, blood pump silenced.
For peace of mind, Midas
should have chosen silver, not gold.

Past littered with poems,
such is her seduction,
her orbit is paved with aspiration,
we still press our suit, seek moon favours.

Too late: virginity lost,

just one small step –

romance has bowed to commodity.

Rival nations set up fiefdoms,

boundaries, rules.

Prospectors mine rare earths,

diggers strip the gleam in her eye,

send it home.

Reduced to a staging post,

rockets countdown to outer space.

Cold rock, she still holds secret:

where gravity thieves time,

lunar conundra,

astronauts age faster.

Nevertheless, she is ruler of the tides,

her French kiss pulls the sea

into embrace; even when unseen,

oceans bulge.

PHOEBE CALDWELL

But for me here,

the moon is queen of night,

her greatest gift, tranquillity.

Rising Banks

The stream is delicate,
picks its way with precision
– shall I wet this side of the boulder
or trickle down the other? –
stone-by-stone deliberation,
highlights hesitant to be written.

After the storm upstream
water strong-arms through my ears,
roars like a rutting stag
as it plunges over the lip:
mesmerised banks
rise as it falls.

Online Syzygy

When you and me double up,
each and each share unseen space:
the meld is greater than our parts.

Together we feel through smoked glass,
yoked minds probing alignment,
throwing out filaments of light
to the shadows of undermind,
solar dragons firing flares into night:
one plus one equals three.
We laugh as we break apart.

Taraxacum Officianalis

Brazen plants: Taraxacums
thrust their heads between cracks,
from seed-dark, discard teguments,
climb to a slit of light
between roadway and pavement.

With the same urgency as the stallion
scents a mare in season,
so dandelions force the gradient,
scrum down urge to procreation,
against tarmac and concrete

to illumination, seed spread,
achene lift-off by parachute,
delicate pappus distribution,
floating on uplift,
sunbursts in my garden.

PHOEBE CALDWELL

Samaritan

like the itinerant on the road
who turned aside and bound the wounds
of a traveller lying in the gutter

like the man who broke his night journey
crawled into the wreckage of a van
and used his thigh to cushion the head
of a woman dangling upside down

deluded or not
like the man who placed his shoulder
under the crossbar of world pain

like those who pause and listen
put aside what they had in mind
lift burdens and with no gain
offer kindness to strangers

we are all strangers to each other
few are from Samaria.

Not To Be Resuscitated

NTBR. It all looks a bit
different to when you made
the decision not to come back
– to now, when you're flat out
on a trolley in the lift,
on the way to surgery,
watching the second hand
tick – knowing they may be
the last ones you'll be abo…

But this time they're not.

Phrenologist

Read my head: know who I am,
feel humours in its humps and bumps,
in the topography of mental states
that reflect my personality
(entered at Stationers Hall):
selfishness at the back,
acquisition to the left,
intuition right, etc. etc.

On the top shelf, you sit next to
the green and red bust of Aristotle,
one-off mould, painted regardless,
from the colourful row of gnomes,
on the table in an occupational
therapy department. Philosopher
and Mistake, what do you talk about?

Labour

The evening pauses,
heaves a sigh of relief,
opens its pores
to let the land drain;
some storm, that was.

No flashy lightning
blowing its fuses, just thunder
rumbling on and on,
hills echoing all afternoon;
interminable rain, rain

like you've never seen,
monsoon break,
cloud sluice bearing down
in continuous spasm:
earth born again.

PHOEBE CALDWELL

Mushroom Farm

Ripe compost lines the drive
berms you can smell a mile off.

Echoes bounce off the walls,
Jack-hammer noise and heat
saturate the factory.
Clean cans feed from overhead,
clash, jostle, crash. Steam pressure
rapes the women's ears.
Hands in Black Sliced,
they shout to each other,
after a time, go deaf.

A cleaner sweeps up fag-ends
from the toilet floor, tips them
onto the moving belt,
anything too foul is passed.

Surprisingly, the armpits
of a passing boiler lad
trail come-hither sweetness.

But everyone, even the manager
hates Quality Control.

Wearing white coats, our job
is to open up the tins and count
the maggots of the cecid fly.

Bane of intensive mushroom farms,
too many, and we stop the line,
release the product from Canadian trade
to our own, holding up production:
the Canucks are more fussy
than we are at home.

Posh meal. My neighbour condescends.
'And what's your line of work?'
I hesitate, then tell him, word for word.

PHOEBE CALDWELL

He gulps, puts down his knife and fork, inspects his plate of stroganoff.

Conversation over.

Laboratory

Her brain is a lab rat,
finding its way
through a preset maze,
following scent paths,
turning back at dead ends,
learning from errors.

But her mind
is an echolocating bat,
sending out waves
to trap faint whispers,
to mull on the auras of ideas,
sounding boards for intention,
fresh pathways over pre-seeded.

She floats on her back
in rich darkness.

PHOEBE CALDWELL

Nan

Dad in the forces, often abroad,
Nan was my nurse, not Gran, weighed down
by superstitions, armoured in credulity,
which she passed on to me:
Of course I know it's not unlucky
to pull my vest on back to front,
but still check which way round it is,
just in case.

Mostly it was keeping the devil at bay,
knock wood, toss spilled salt
over my left shoulder, catch Old Nick
unawares, gaff him in the eye,
unlucky to break mirrors, walk beneath
a ladder (something to do with triangles
and the Holy Trinity, not sure why):
less diabolical, if you crack the bottom
of a hard-boiled egg, sailors won't drown.

And luck drains from inverted horseshoes,
vulva of Diana, pagan goddess of the moon.
She didn't tell me that one.

Issued by Pope Gregory the Ninth,
black cats came in for a torrid time,
burned alive: papal bull proclaimed
they embodied the soul of Beelzebub.

Aged eight, my faith in her strange beliefs
began to wane when I crossed the Atlantic
to discover that, unlucky back home,
they conveyed good fortune
in the States. Could they be both?
Could Satan not swim?

PHOEBE CALDWELL

Intruder

You could hardly call it
a waterfall, only a few tears
wrung from stonedraught,
thin trickle over a lip
into the valley below,
just enough to wet my face
at high noon.

A monster hornet passes
at eye level, following
a predetermined flight path –
it knows where it's going,
I am stranger to its territory.

Needing shelter from the sun,
I squeeze into a crevice, turn
to see it's already occupied –
a black and white tail
slides further in; I am not alone.

Plato's Poet

I've flirted with philosophers,
too serious, no room
for laughs; in heaven
never quite made the front row.

So bring me a comfy chair,
sit me behind
in Plato's second line
where no-one will notice
my nightly compulsion
to let down the net,
trawl the undermind,
tease out what's there.

PHOEBE CALDWELL

Leafprint

Smear on the ground, the only one left,

Sycamore palm print fading to mulch,

nearly a year since you broke bud, unfurled,

setting your foil to the sun's beam, factory
    part

in a gas-conversion scheme,

working all daylight hours.

Worn-out Stakhanovite, an October wind

tore you down, settled you on the path,

masthead to earth in one gust,

print without substance, recalling the shape

of a hand with splayed fingers scorched on
    paving:

Hiroshima etched in the mind.

Camouflage

Big I hides round the corner
under a scarf, T-shirt rolls, a hat,
or in the wastepaper basket,
spies from splayed fingers,
peeps from her mask.

Small i is on the alert,
ready to duck at first sign
of threat, obliterate face:
if I cannot see you,
you can't see me.

As hard as she tries,
I's paintbrush will out
the signature of self.

PHOEBE CALDWELL

Chronology

Tick-tock, tick-tock, tick-tock,
Newton or Einstein, absolute time
or nearly so, faster up there
than here on Earth: Pisa
opens its ground-floor door
to listen to what happened up top
a slither of a minisec past; real time
tethered to a trapped-ion clock
watches caesium atoms jump.

Grandfather Time hobbles
out of sync; morning and evening
play hopscotch, collide,
behaving like cardigan buttons
pushed through inapposite slots,
two sides done up,
but a lived-in, misfitting
analogue droop.

(Einstein's Relativity demonstrated that Time is not a constant but dependent on the gravitational pull due to distance from the centre of the Earth. It'd be faster the further you get from the centre of the Earth.)

Astrophysical Lexicon

Holographic World: Space-Time
squashed flat, hiding inside Black Holes
beyond Horizon Events –
except for the odd string leaked out;
so dense, both happenings –
and words to describe them,
are inscrutable, offline.

A thingummy language, neonate,
cut to fit new branches of science,
Quantum Wave particle dualities
pinpoint either or both,
depending how they are read.
Superposition: one item
in multiple states. Uncertainty:
not sure which, only a single
perspective, say, position or speed,
can be logged at a time.

Entanglement scrambles the brain:
on opposite sides of the world,
A triggers A – no apparent connection,
two separate objects behave with one mind.

Comprehension struggles and some,
better go back to knitting,
one plain, one purl, jumper
straight off the cliff. Cast off.

Getting To Know Alexa

Plug in. Start with her name.
'Alexa, let's have fun,
tell me a joke!'
She comes back with a pun –
'Duck in hospital,
put the doctor's fee on the bill' –
all the wild mirth
of a geothermal mud puddle
burping air, slow delivery,
flat outcome.

Sharing camaraderie with AI
is problematical.

Time Out of Sync

An old woman pauses by the recycling bins
for rest, for reflection.

Before the Leeds Liverpool Canal
ran out of funds, this car park, and the rugby
    pitch

would have been the terminus for barges.
She would have had space

to sit and think – or just sit –
watching horsepower churn the water,

dozing on a wooden bench,
as the long-boats turn, headed back to port.

Angus Again

Angus was born with a smile
on his face, he looks round the room
for someone to help him bang bricks.
When he catches their gaze,
it's more than a Cheshire Cat grin,
His eyes light up,
from the standing wave
of his topmost curl to his
'piggy went to market' wriggling toes,
his whole body joins in,
an invitation to play with him.

With love from his great-granny

Sheltered Housing

In the old folks' home
her flat overlooks streetlights.
Lights come on automatically
when she steps outside her door.
There's no corridor
where she can stand in darkness
and gaze into the unblinking eye
of the blue moon.

PHOEBE CALDWELL

Death

She said to her daughter one day,
'The great thing about being dead,
you don't have to get up and pee
in the night,' to which she replied,
'Even better; no need to get out of bed.'

Yahweh

Ashes to ash, worm food, when I'm gone
there'll be no me, not me, at best a few ideas,
brief shadows in an aftermath.

Alive, I'm weighed down, crooked as the top
    half
of a question mark, defined by pronouns,
tethered to preference and identity.

He, she or it, shall I in afterwards or not,
meet an unmet God I know but cannot;
the unassigned continuum, I AM?

PHOEBE CALDWELL

Bookworms

Stone figures
buried in a book
lean out of their headstones,
grow from the ground.

Noses in the page,
he and she do not
look up at passers-by,
mere death cannot
interrupt a good story.

*(These two delightful tombstones are in the
graveyard of Dryburgh Abbey on the banks of
the River Tweed on the Scottish borders.)*

Dropped Catch

(A gold-and-red painting of 'The Fall of Icarus'
by James Martin hangs on my bedroom wall.
James said that it was an 'awkward squad' of
angels sent to save Icarus. He was also allergic
to feathers, so in his painting, Icarus' wings are
made of leaves, not feathers.

After some legal wrangling, a bronze statue of
Icarus is being returned to its original site in the
grounds of Leighton Hall. As a child, I stayed
with my cousin G. (Naylor?) who had been a
suffragette, in Leighton Hall during the panic
war in 1939.)

Daedalus and his son escape from the
    labyrinth,

King Minos and the minotaur hide in a bush.

While his dad builds wings from feathers and
    beeswax,

he councils the boy, 'Listen,

PHOEBE CALDWELL

Do not fly too high, or the heat of the sun
will melt the wax and you'll fall.' Deaf to his
    plea,
Icarus can't wait to take off.
Together they stand on the cliff edge,
flap hard and jump into nothingness.

Up and away, Icarus leaves his dad behind,
ignores the chafe of his wings,
dodges the odd bits of space junk,
soars into the void.

The heat increases, a solar flare explodes
into plasma plumes, Icarus' wings deliquesce,
oil runs, his feathers wither,
fall like autumn leaves, he plunges
back through the stratosphere.

Swifter than light, gravity drags him down.
Earth comes nearer, panic sets in
as his parachute fails to open.
Sent to capture his headlong dive,

inattentive angels, gripping a Persian rug,
fail to intercept his fatal plummet.
Icarus crashes to doom.

And lands, nose first
(wings suspiciously intact),
in the serpentine pond
of a castle in mid Wales,
bronze statue returning to its original site.

Journey through space and time
squeezed into one, from Greek mythology
to the mind of painter, James Martin,
and sculptor, Hippolyte, full circle
to the grounds of Leighton Hall,
where (playing cricket as a child)
the poet dropped a catch. Here now,
after legal outs and ins, Icarus,
the boy who flew too high, comes home.

PHOEBE CALDWELL

Gaza

Three thousand years ago
King Alexander
and his Macedonian troops
assaulted the soaring walls of Gaza,
building mounds to aim siege engines.
Winner third time round,
he slaughtered the men, sold
the women and children into slavery:
collateral damage on the way to Egypt.

Imprisoned in Gaza, Samson,
Nazirite, feasted with a Philistine,
broke his mother's vow,
could not resist the lure of Delilah –
the secret of his strength
grew in his uncut hair. While he slept
she scissored his head:
bald, he was weak as other men.

'As if', the premise for 'suppose',

a kissing gate swings to 'possibility':

any chance the broken curse

was handed down?

From Alexander on,

a punchball city has been seized,

razed to the ground, staggered

to its feet again as the tide of nations,

tribes, infidels and believers

ebbed and flowed, pounding to rubble

the memories of those who came before.

Ancient Egyptian, Canaan, Hyksos,

Egypt again, Philistines, Hebrews,

neo-Assyrians, and the try-once-more

Egyptians, neo-Babylonians, Achaemenids,

Macedonians, Ptolemaics and Seleucids:

all eyes on a city built astride

the north-south trade route –

and that was before the Romans came:

King Herod, designate, brought interim
     peace
until that empire crumbled.

Saladin and the Crusaders
used Gaza as their tiltyard.

Over and above antagonists,
this stricken city has been
battered by earthquakes,
feasted on by locusts and endured
the pustules of bubonic plague.
A leap in time brings Gaza up to date,
straight-line conflict between Arabs
and Israelis. No more, see the fear you kill,
smart phones launch push-button war,
remote-control rockets and unmanned
     drones
sandwich blocks of flats, burying
stay-at-home women and children.
Seeking tunnels underground,

misfires from either side send
arbitrary strikes on churches,
mosques, hospitals and schools:
more simply, starve them out.
Mutual distrust and hatred
devours innocents.

When will this bring an end?

Dandelions

They are bold, these plants

that thrust heads between cracks,

from seed-dark, discarding teguments,

climbing the gradient towards a slit of light

between roadway and pavement.

Groundsel and occasional

hedge parsley, the spindly sort,

but mostly, brazen-headed

Taraxacum Officianalis. (Daisies

and clover prefer open grass.)

As the stallion yearns

for a mare in season, so

dandelions force the gradient,

scrum down urge to procreation

against tarmac and concrete

to illumination, seed spread,
achene lift-off by parachute,
delicate pappus distribution,
floating miles on the breeze,
sunbursts in my garden.

Jo

Editor, reviewer, trader,
friend, in answer to queries,
she always replied, 'Yes,
I think I can lay my hands
on that one,' disappeared
into a labyrinth of paperbacks
stacked against her walls,
returning, 'By the way,
did you know...?'

In her nest of books,
Jo has always seemed
frail as a bird,
now she's gone, grief
is ours to live.

Escaped from Prague

Deep country, one of those banked-up lanes
burnished with gorse, tipping out on a green:
a pottery on the further side,
platters and plaques in casual display
all over the grass. Potter away, anyone
could have helped themselves.

I leave my number, he rings back,
his voice is soft when he calls,
'To whom have I the honour of speaking?'

His plate sits on the table in my hall,
heads of a woman and man, eyes lost
in the other, lips fired, anticipation
in the timeless quiver before kiss.

My mother would have left
a calling card to hide their bliss,

PHOEBE CALDWELL

for me, its mundane stuff, door keys,

blue badges and a pile of clean laundry,

waiting to be put away in the drawer,

but I know they are there underneath.

Grammatical Shift

Squeezed between pity and presumption

there's a special lowest-common-
    denominator voice

shifting pronouns from direct to indirect,

patronising old-speak through a dusty
    window –

'Would she like…?' 'Did she want…?'
    spoken sideways

as if she were not there, over-her-head crafted
    conditional

pseudo-sympathetic, to humour the poor
    dear.

She may be wheelchair-bound, marbles
    rattling

occasionally while she conducts a tip-of-the-
    tongue

databank search, but she is still subject with
    history,

not child. Wait until you get there.

PHOEBE CALDWELL

For Ever

When time stops

there will be no

sequences,

before and after,

anticipation of the future,

recollection of the past,

only suspended now.

The pack will remain

unshuffled.

Is this eternity?

Never Go Back

History is a movable feast:
memories are now, in the lane
where you asked me to marry you,
more of a track, Clwyds
on the skyline, your invitation
close up. All gone now,
buried under a development,
no trace of our tryst.

Further back to the house
Dad built, next door
to the smuggler's cottage.
Climbing ladders to the first floor,
he forgot to put in stairs. Wide views
embraced the South Downs,
marshland and sea. At the end
of the field, oyster catchers
nested in blackberry thickets.

PHOEBE CALDWELL

Trees felled, hedges with primroses
and violets subsumed beneath
foundations: time slipped builds
housing estates over the past.

About the Author

Phoebe Caldwell is an expert practitioner and creator of the 'Responsive Communication' approach and has worked for more than fifty years with people on the autism spectrum. She is the published author of fourteen books on autism, the most recent combining best practice with contemporary neurobiological research, and four books on ageing. Together with Janet Gurney, she produced a major training film and has won the Times Sternberg Award for her work. In 2011, she was awarded an honorary Doctorate of Science. Now in her nineties, Phoebe is still working via Zoom and says she is a poet 'by accident'.

Website: https://www.phoebecaldwell.com

For more titles from Beaten Track Publishing, please visit our website:

https://www.beatentrackpublishing.com

Thanks for reading!

www.ingramcontent.com/pod-product-compliance
Lightning Source LLC
Chambersburg PA
CBHW060038040426
42331CB00032B/1212